Stocks

Growth

Stability

Risk

By

Mito Bessalel

Author's Rights

Stock Growth Stability Risk

This book is sold with the understanding than the author and publisher(s) are not providing advice of any nature, to individuals, institutions or companies.

Table of Contents

Chapter 1 - Introduction

1.1 Concept

Early this summer I attended a seminar in one of the Fidelity Investment branch. The purpose of the seminar was to help investors improve their knowledge concerning the use of the fundamental and technical analysis to study market data of a selected stock.

The instructor explained the basis of the Fundamental Analysis (**FA**) and the Technical Analysis (**TA**).

I understood the technology behind the **FA** and all the parameters to determine the performance of a company, so investors might understand how to analyze and purchase stocks.

I also understood the use of existing data to make predictions using opening and closure of stocks during a period of time and how the **TA** manipulates graphic data from charts to create indexes and parameters to study future behavior of stocks.

Those analyses if they are well understood could assist investors to select stocks that could provide profit. However, none of the two analyses give a predicted future of stock price or detail of growth, stability and risk.

GSRMM will process the collected input data and output the following:

a. Growth index (**GI**)
b. Stability Index (**SI**)
c. Risk Index (**RI**)

1.2 The Growth, Stability and Risk Mathematical Model

The software of the Growth, Stability and Risk mathematical model includes the following.

a. Growth software
b. Stability software
c. Risk software

The input data required to run GSRMM was extracted from the 2013 and 2012 Annual reports.

1.2.1 GSRMM Outputs the Growth Index

GSRMM will process the following input data and output the Growth Index.

a. Sales growth
b. Income Growth
c. Net Profit Marginal

Sales Growth

It is a measure of the **percentage increase in** sales between two periods.

Income growth

It is a measure of the percentage increases between two periods.

Net Profit Marginal

Managers should view growth rate of net income to determine if their firm is growing at a sustainable level.

The input data was obtained from www.msn.com/money.

1.2.2 GSRMM Outputs the Stability Index

GSRMM will process the following input data and will output the Stability Index.

Input Data

   a. Revenues per share
   b. Earning per share
   c. Beta
   d. Debt/Equity
   e. Average opinion of the analysts

Revenues per share

Includes the total revenues earned per share over a 12-month period. It is calculated by dividing total revenue earned in a fiscal year by the weighted average of shares outstanding for that fiscal year.

Earning per share

Measures the efficiency of the company it serves as an indicator of a company's profitability.

Beta

Measure the volatility, or the systematic risk of a security in comparison to the market as a whole.

Debt/equity ratio
Measure the relative contribution of the creditors and shareholders or owners in the capital employed in **business**.

The input data can be obtained from www.msn.com/money and www.yahoo.com/finaces.

1.2.3 GSRMM Outputs the Risk Index

GRSMM will process the following input data and output the Risk Index.

Input Data
  a. 52 weeks high
  b. 52 weeks low
  c. Current stock opening
  d. Beta
  e. Debt/Equity
  f. Revenues per share
  g. Earning per share

52 Weeks high and Low
Level prices that a stock traded at during the
previous year; both are important factors in
determining a stock's current value and for
predicting future price movements.

Current stock Opening
Is the price of the stock open the day the analysis
was performed.
Beta, see 1.22
Debt/Equity; see 1.2.2
Revenues per share; see 1.2.2
Earning per share; 1see 1.2.2

The input data for the Risk Index can be obtained
from www.msn.com/money and
www.yahoo.com/finaces.

1.2.4 Moving Averages

GSRMM output the following

 a. 5 days moving average
 b. 10 days moving average
 c. 50 days moving average
 d. 200 days moving average

The moving averages should help the reader to
understand the stock performance and help to
purchase and sales stocks.

Chapter 2 Input Data

2.1 Input data for Growth, Stability and Risks Indexes

The Input data required to run the model was selected based on the function of the indexes to be analyzed by GSRMM. The input data shown below were extracted from the Johnson and Johnson annual report of June 13, 2014.

Table 1
Input data for Growth, Stability and Risk Indexes

Stock	JNJ
Data was gathered	6/13/2014
Year when data was gathered	2014
Stock was opened when data was gathered	102.52
Dividends	2.73
52 weeks high	104.15
52 weeks low	82.12
Sales growth	6.10
Income Growth	27.40
Net Marginal Profit	20.94
Debt/equity	0.23

Beta	0.56
Earnings per Share (EPS)	5.23
Forward P/E	16.17
Trailing P/E	19.61
Stock open at the beginning of the year	91.14
Revenues per share	25.52
Analysts 'mean opinion	2.40

2.2-Input data for Moving Averages

Table 2

Input data for 50 and 200 days moving averages

50 days moving average	101.26
200 days moving average	95.67

Table 3 –

Stocks Opening for the last 10 days

Stock	JNJ
Day 1	102.51
Day 2	103.18
Day 3	103.81
Day 4	103.47
Day 5	103.07
Day 6	103.25
Day 7	102.78
Day 8	102.33
Day 9t	101.91
Day 10	101.54

Chapter 3 Designing GSRMM

This chapter details step by step the design of the software to output the Growth, Sensitivity and Risk index and stock projections Excel 2010 was used to develop **GSRMM.**

3.1-Growth software

Step 1
Collect the Input data:
  a. Sales growth
  b. Income growth
  c. Net profit Margin

Step 2
Plot the input data in XY Coordinate System

Table 4 shows the detail how the Growth input data is entered in XY coordinate system. See figure 1.

Table 4 – Growth Input data in a XY coordinate system

Point	Angle from X	Value
A	0	a
B	120	b
C	240	c

a. Segment OA = Sales growth
b. Segment OB = Income growth
c. Segment OC –Profit Net Profit

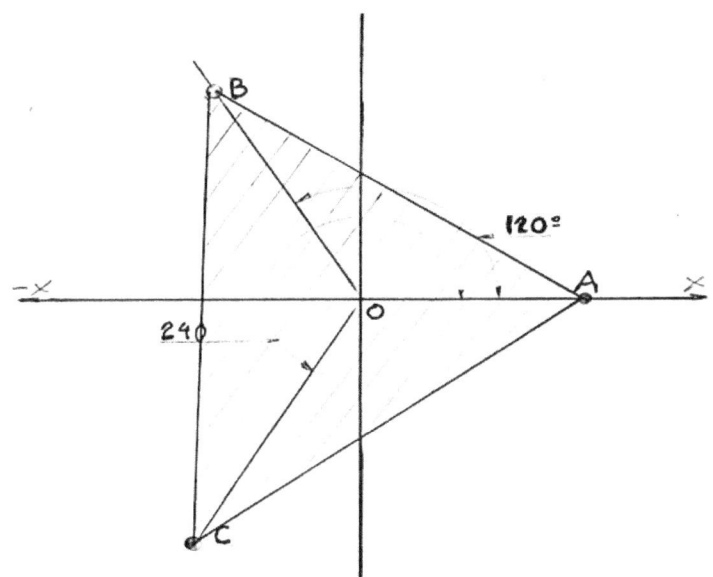

Figure 1 - Triangular Mathematical Model

Step 3
Surface of triangle ABC

Using the cross multiplication method, GRSMM calculates the surface of triangle ABC.

The coordinates for the vertices are

For point A=Xa/Ya
For point B=Xb/Yb
For point C=Xc/Yc

Find the surface of the triangle using cross multiplication method

$$S=(Xa*Yb+Xb*Yb+Xc*Ya-$$
$$(Xa*Yc+Xc*Yb+Xb*Ya)/2$$

Growth index =Surface of the triangle ABD

3.2 Stability Software

Step 1
Collect the Input data

 a. Revenues per share
 b. Earnings per share
 c. Debt/Equity
 d. Beta
 e. Average opinion of the analysts

Step2

GSRMM calculates the difference between the revenue per share and earning per share.

h=revenues/share-earning per share

Step 3

Plotting the input data in XY Coordinate System

Table5 – Sensitivity Input data in a XY coordinate system

Point	Angle from X	Value
A	0	h
B	90	b
C	180	c
D	270	d

Segment OA= h

Segment OB =b

Segment OC= c

Segment OD=d

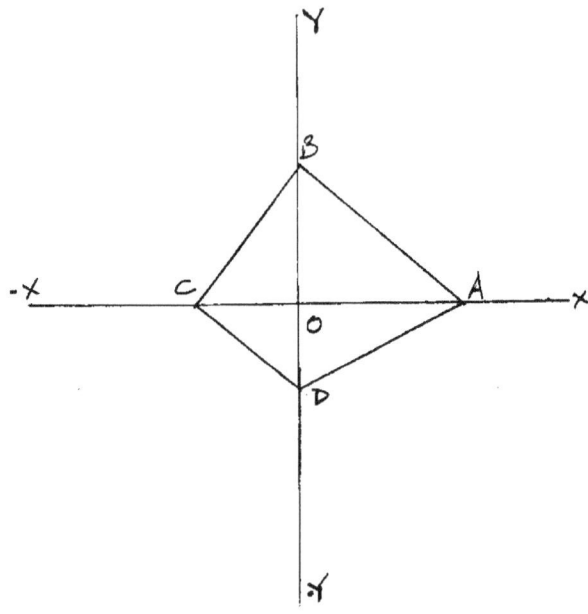

Figure 2 Rectangular Mathematical Model

Step 4
Surface of rectangle
GSRMM calculates the area of the rectangle as follows

The surface of rectangle is equal to the area of triangle ABD plus the area of the triangle ACD.

Surface of rectangle= surface of ABC+surface ACD

Stability index = surface of rectangle ABCD

3.3 Risk Software

Step 1
Input data

    a. 52 weeks high
    b. 52 weeks low
    c. Current opening
    d. Return per share
    e. Debt/ Equity
    f. Beta
    g. Earning per share

Step2

GRSMM finds the following radios:

h=52 weeks high/52 weeks low
g= current opening/52 weeks low

j=revenues per share/earning per share

Step 3

Plotting the input data in XY Coordinate System

Table 6– Sensitivity Input data in a XY coordinate system

Point	Angle from X	Value
A	0	h
B	72	G
C	144	J
D	216	d
E	288	e

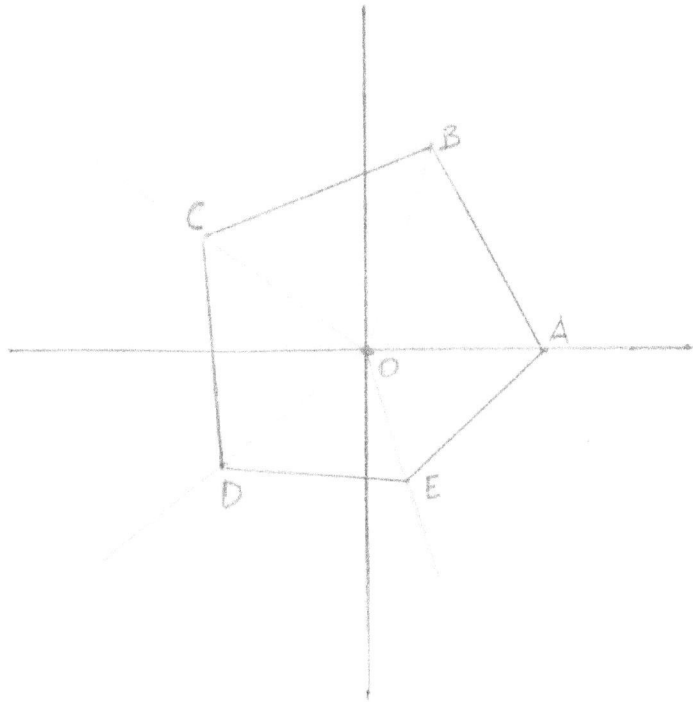

Figure 3 Pentagon Mathematical model

Segment OA= h
Segment OB =g
Segment OC= j
Segment OD=d
Segment OE=e

Step 5

Using the cross multiplication method GSRMM calculates the surface of the pentagon ABCDE.

Coordinate of the vertexes of the pentagon are

A=Xa/Ya
B=Xb/Yb
C=Xc/Yc
D=Xd/Yd
E=Xe/YE

 Surface of pentagon

P= Xa*Yb +Xb*Yc + X c*Yd + Xd*Ye + Xe*Ya
R=Xa*Ye + Xe*Yd + Xd*Ye + Xc*Yb + Xb*Ya
Surface =(P-R)/2
RI=surface of ABCDE

3.4 Moving averages

Collect the following input data

Stock Growth Stability Risk

    a. 50 days average data
    b. 200 days average data
    c. Last 10 stocks open (section 2.2)

CSRMM outputs
    a. 5 day moving average
    b. 10 days moving average
    c. 50 days moving average
    d. 200 days moving average

Chapter 4 – Running GRSMM

In this chapter GSRMM process the input data for Johnson &Johnson for June 13 2014 and different input data.

4.1 Growth Index

Scenario 1

Input data for June 13

Sale growth	6.10
Income Growth	27.40
Net Profit Market	20.94

GRSMM outputs the Growth Index

GI = 37.61

Running GRSMM for different input data

Scenario2

Assuming sales growth =O

Input data

Sale growth	0
Income Growth	27.40
Net Profit Market	20.94

Growth Index=24.84

Scenario 3

Assuming Income growth =*0*

Input data

Sale growth   6.10

Income Growth   *0*

Net Profit Market   20.94

Growth index = 5.43

Scenario 4

Assuming sales growth and income growth are equal cero

Input data

Sale growth   *0*

Income Growth   *0*

Net Profit Market   20.94

Growth index =0

Table 7 Growth Index Scenarios – Summary

Scenario	1	2	3	4
Sales Growth	6.10	*0*	6.10	*0*
Income	27.40	27.40	0	*0*

Growth				
Net Profit Margin	20.94	20.94	20.94	20.94
Growth Index	37.64	24.84	*5.430*	*0*

4.2 Stability Index

Scenario 1
Input data for June 13

Revenues per share = 25.52
Earning per share = 5.23
Beta = 0.56
Debt/Equity = 0.23
Analysts opinion medium = 2.40
Stability Index = 30.37

Scenario 2
Assuming earning per share =*10.00*
Input data
Revenues per share = =25.52
Earning per share =*10.00*
Beta =0.56
Debt/equity =0.23

Analyst opinion	=2.40
Stability Index	= 23.31

Scenario 3
Assuming Beta= 1.50
Input data

Revenues per share =	=25.52
Earning per share	=5.23
Beta	=1.50
Debt/equity	=0.23
Analyst opinion	=2.40
Stability Index	=40.02

Scenario 4
Assuming Analysts' opinion =1

Revenues per share =	=25.52
Earning per share	=5.23
Beta	=O.56
Debt/equity	=0.23
Analyst opinion	=1.00
Stability Index	= 16.01

able 8 Stability Analyses – Summary

Scenario	1	2	3	4
Revenues per share	25.52	25.52	25.53	25.53
Return per share	5.23.	*10.00*	5.23	5.23
Beta	0.56	0.56	*1.50*	0.56
Debt/equity	0.23	0.23	0.23	0.23
Analyst Ave. opinion	2.40	2.40	1.00	*1.00*
Stability Index	30.37	23.31	40.02	16.01

Conclusion, smaller stability index represents better company management.

4.3 Risk Index

Scenario 1
Input data for June 13

52 weeks high   =104.15
52 weeks low   = 82.12
Stock open   =102.51
Revenues per share   = 25.52
Earning per share   =   5.23

Stock Growth Stability Risk

Beta	=	0.56
Debt/Equity	=	0.23
Risk Index	=	6.27

Scenario 2

Assumption: 52 weeks low =100.00

Input data

52 weeks high	=104.15
52 weeks low	=*100.00*
Stock open	=102.51
Revenues per share	= 25.52
Earning per share	= 5.23
Beta	= 0.56
Debt/Equity	= 0.23
Risk Index	= 6.05

Scenario 3

Assumption Earning per share =10

Input data

52 weeks high	=104.15
52 weeks low	= 82.12
Stock open	=102.51
Revenues per share	= 25.52
Earning per share	= *10.00*
Beta	= 0.56
Debt/Equity	= 0.23
Risk Index	= 3.39

Scenario 4

Assumption: 52 weeks low =100.00

Input data

52 weeks high	=104.15
52 weeks low	= 82.12
Stock open	=102.51
Revenues per share	= 25.52
Earning per share	= 5.23
Beta	= 0.56
Debt/Equity	= *1.00*
Risk Index	= 0.56

Table 9 Risk Analyses – Summary

Scenario	1	2	3	4
52 weeks High	104.15	104.15	104.15	104.15
52 weeks low	81.12.	*100.00*	81.12	82.12
Stock Open	102.51	102.51	102.51	102.51
Revenues per share	25.52	25.52	25.52	25.52
Earnings per share	5.23	5.23	*10.00*	5.23
Beta	0.56	0.56	0.56	0.56
Debt/Equity	0.23	0.23	0.23	*1.00*
Risk index	6.27	6.05	3.39	*0.56*

Conclusion, smaller risk index represents better company management.

4.4 Moving Averages

Step 1

   a. 50 days moving average = 101.26

   b. 200 days moving average = 95.67

   c. Opening for the last 10 days

      Day 1 = 102.51

      Day 2 = 103.18

      Day 3 = 103.81

      Day 4 = 103.47

      Day 5 = 103.07

      Day 6 = 103.25

      Day 7 = 102.78

      Day 8 = 102.23

      Day 9 = 101.91

      Day 10 = 101.54

Step 2

Stock Growth Stability Risk

Enter in sheet "Input " the collected data and find the 5 y 10 days average moving indicators.

Step 3

GSRMM outputs

a. 5 days moving average =103.15
b. 10 days moving average = 102.74
c. 50 days moving average = 101.26
d. 200 days moving averages = 95.67

Chapter 5 – GSRMM Applications

As indicated in Chapter I the purpose of this is to assist investors to analyze 3 indexes. The following scenarios will be analyzed using CSRMM:

a. Citigroup run for &/16/2014 (C)
b. Johnson and Johnson run 6/13/2014 (JNJ)
c. Johnson and Johnson run for 7/11/2014 (JNJ)
d. Microsoft run for 7/15/2014 (MSFT)
e. Micron run for 7/14/2014 (MU)
f. National Oilwell Varco, Inc. 7/15/2014 (NOW)
g. AT & T run for &/16/2014 (T)
h. Compare output for JNJ
i. Compare two companies

5.1 One Company for two different dates

In this section we will collect the input data for JNJ for

a. June 13 2014
b. July 11 2014
c. Compare runs

5.1.1 Input - Output data for JNJ for June 13

Input

Stock	JNJ
Data was collected	6/13/2014
Year when data was gathered	2014
Stock was opened when data was gathered	102.51
Dividends	2.73
52 weeks high	104.15
52 weeks low	82.12
Sales growth	6.10
Income Growth	27.40
Net Marginal Profit	20.94
Debt/equity	0.23
Beta	0.56
Earnings per Share (EPS)	5.23
Forward P/E	16.17
Trailing P/E	19.61
Stock open at the beginning of the year	91.14
Revenues per share	25.52
Analysts 'mean opinion	2.40
50 days moving average	101.26
200 days moving average	95.67

Output Indexes

Growth Index	37.61
Stability Index	30.37
Risk Index	6.77

Output Moving average

5 days moving average	103.15
10 days moving average	102.74
50 days moving average	101.26
200 days moving average	95.67

5.1.2 Input and output for NJN for July 11, 2014

Input

Stock	JNJ
Data was collected	7/11/2014
Year when data was gathered	2014
Stock was opened when data was gathered	105.10
Dividends	2.65
52 weeks high	106.75
52 weeks low	85.50
Sales growth	6.10
Income Growth	27.40
Net Marginal Profit	20.94
Debt/equity	0.23
Beta	0.56
Earnings per Share (EPS)	5.23
Forward P/E	16.60
Trailing P/E	19.61
Stock open at the beginning of the year	91.14
Revenues per share	25.52
Analysts 'mean opinion	2.40
50 days moving average	103.73
200 days moving average	97.30

Stock Growth Stability Risk

Output Data

Growth Index	37.61
Stability Index	30.37
Risk Index	6.77

Output Moving average

5 days moving average	105.71
10 days moving average	105.64
50 days moving average	103.72
200 days moving average	97.30

5.1.3 Compare 2 runs for Johnson and Johnson

June and July JNJ runs

Stock	JNJ	JNJ
Data was collected	6/13/2014	7/11/2014
Year when data was gathered	2014	2014
Stock opened when data was Collected	102.52	105.10
Dividends	2.73	2.65
52 weeks high	104.15	106.74
52 weeks low	82.12	85.50
Sales growth	6.10	6.10
Income Growth	27.40	27.40
Net Marginal Profit	6.37	6.37
Debt/equity	0.23	0.23
Beta	0.56	0.56
Earnings per Share (EPS)	5.23	5.23
Forward P/E	16.17	16.60
Trailing P/E	19.61	20.10
Stock open at the	91.14	91.14

beginning of the year		
Revenues per share	25.52	25.52
Analysts 'mean opinion	2.40	2.40
50 days moving average	101.26	103.72
200 days moving average	95.67	97.30

Output Data

Growth Index	37.61	37.61
Stability Index	30.37	*30.37*
Risk Index	6.77	6.77

Output Moving average

5 days moving average	103.15	105.71
10 days moving average	102.74	105.64
50 days moving average	103.26	103.72
200 days moving average	96.67	97.30

5.2 July 16 Input and output data for Citigroup(C)

Input

Stock	C
Data was collected	7/16/2014
Year when data was gathered	2014
Stock was opened when data was gathered	49.49
Dividends	0.10
52 weeks high	55.28
52 weeks low	45.18
Sales growth	8.00
Income Growth	74.30
Net Marginal Profit	17.95
Debt/equity	1.40
Beta	1.88
Earnings per Share (EPS)	4.35
Forward P/E	9.516
Trailing P/E	11.46
Stock open at the beginning of the year	52.03
Revenues per share	22.47
Analysts 'mean opinion	2.10

Output Data

Growth Index	82.11
Stability Index	38.84
Risk Index	18.18

Output Moving average

200 days moving average	48.16
50 days moving average	47.45
10 days moving average	47.98
5 days moving average	48.10

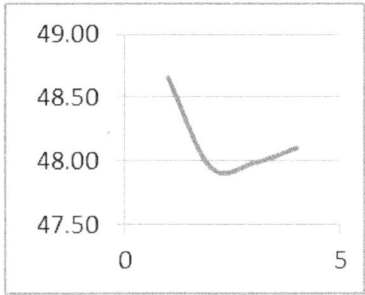

Figure 4 moving averages for C

5.3 July 15 Input and output data for Microsoft Corporation (MSFT

Input

Stock	MSFT
Data was collected	7/15/2014
Year when data was gathered	2014
Stock was opened when data was gathered	42.15
Dividends	2.66
52 weeks high	42.47
52 weeks low	30.84
Sales growth	5.60
Income Growth	28.80
Net Marginal Profit	26.91
Debt/equity	0.26
Beta	0.92
Earnings per Share (EPS)	2.66
Forward P/E	13.6530
Trailing P/E	15.45
Stock open at the beginning of the year	37.35
Revenues per share	10.01
Analysts 'mean opinion	2.65

Output Data

Growth Index	48.27
Stability Index	13.58
Risk Index	6.83

Microsoft - Output Moving average

200 days moving average	39.18
50 days moving average	41.38
10 days moving average	42.12
5 days moving average	42.15

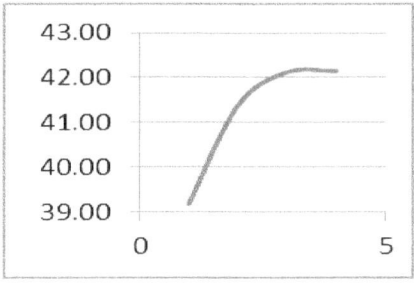

Figure 5 – Microsoft Moing Averages

5.4 July 14 Input and output data for Micron Technology (MU)

Input

Stock	MU
Data was collected	7/14/2014
Year when data was gathered	2014
Stock was opened when data was gathered	33.49
Dividends	0
52 weeks high	34.50
52 weeks low	12.31
Sales growth	10.20
Income Growth	40.80*
Net Marginal Profit	24.06
Debt/equity	0.57
Beta	1.80
Earnings per Share (EPS)	3.03
Forward P/E	11.230
Trailing P/E	11.10
Stock open at the beginning of the year	21.60
Revenues per share	25.5214.24
Analysts 'mean opinion	2.00
50 days moving average	31.06
200 days moving average	25.85

Stock Growth Stability Risk

*No data was given in the annual report, because in 2012, income was negative. However the increment of cash flow growth from 2012 to 2013 was 40.8 %

Output Data

Stock	MU
Growth Index	59.67
Stability Index	22.38
Risk Index	20.33

Output Moving average

200 days moving average	25.85
50 days moving average	31.06
10 days moving average	35.09
5 days moving average	36.78

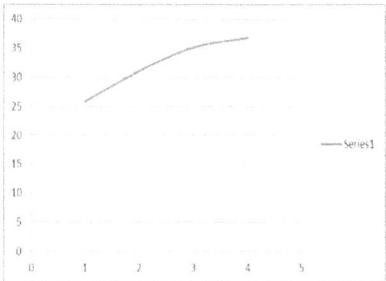

Figure 6 moving averages for MU

5.5 July 16 Input and output data for National Oil wall Varco (NOV)

Input

Stock	NOV
Data was collected	7/16/2014
Year when data was gathered	2014
Stock was opened when data was gathered	84.26
Dividends	2.19
52 weeks high	85.47
52 weeks low	84.17
Sales growth	11.23
Income Growth	3.60
Net Marginal Profit	10.341
Debt/equity	0.14
Beta	1,91
Earnings per Share (EPS)	5.46
Forward P/E	12.16
Trailing P/E	15.16
Stock open at the beginning of the year	79.40
Revenues per share	54.72
Analysts 'mean opinion	1.98

Output Data

Growth Index	5.29
Stability Index	96.08
Risk Index	45.55

Output Moving average

200 days moving average	72.53
50 days moving average	79,42
10 days moving average	83.00
5 days moving average	83.33

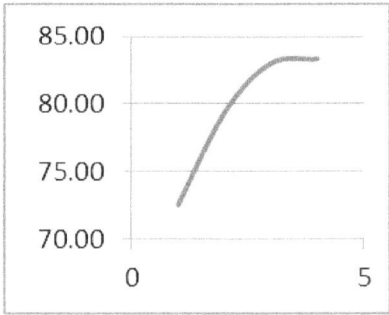

Figure 7 moving averages for NOv

5.6 July 16 Input and output data for AT&T

Input

Stock	T
Data was collected	7/16/2014
Year when data was gathered	2014
Stock was opened when data was gathered	36.45
Dividends	5.20
52 weeks high	36.86
52 weeks low	31.74
Sales growth	1.00
Income Growth	151.20
Net Marginal Profit	14.01
Debt/equity	0.88
Beta	0.29
Earnings per Share (EPS)	3.43
Forward P/E	13.29
Trailing P/E	10.63
Stock open at the beginning of the year	35.24
Revenues per share	24.53
Analysts 'mean opinion	2.7

Stock Growth Stability Risk

Output Data

Growth Index	135.36
Stability Index	36.86
Risk Index	8.08

Output Moving average

200 days moving average	35.30
50 days moving average	36.86
10 days moving average	37.88
5 days moving average	36.86

In Closing

I hope you follow the procedures of the analysis presented in this book and if you feel that the analysis mathematical models used to determine the growth, stability and risk of companies could assist you in any way and would like to obtain a copy of the software to be used in your analysis, please contact the author at:

Bessalel@msn.com

The cost of the CD including the software of the GSRMM Mathematical Model,
CD   5.99 USA Dollar, plus shipping charges
E-Copy   3.99 USA Dollar (Sent via internet)

Please note that all this calculation presented in this publication can be calculated manually.

About the author

Mito Bessalel, PE performed several financial analyses for several cities in Indonesia and industries in The Philippines. Additionally he prepared business plans for the Solid Waste management for several cities in Asia, Africa and Latin America.

He graduated as a civil engineer from the University of Buenos Aires in 1957. He immigrated to USA 6 years after graduation. Five years later he began working worldwide as a consultant. Among his responsibilities he developed several mathematical models as a component of business plans for city planning.

 He worked for institutions like the World Bank, USAID and the African Development Bank.

He lives In Maryland, USA with his wife.

www.ingramcontent.com/pod-product-compliance
Lightning Source LLC
Chambersburg PA
CBHW071646170526
45166CB00003B/1448